THE TOWEL THAT SAVED ELIZABETH

Published by Rhyme Time Publications

Illustrated by Toby Mikle of MyBookIllustrator.com

Note from the Author

Many years ago, nine-year old Lotti saved the life of five-year old Elizabeth. But for Lotti, Elizabeth would have drowned in a deep and dangerous river.

I know this story is true because Lotti is my wife's sister.

Dedicated to

all the young children who often do
brave and important things
all by themselves.

Grandmother Invites Lotti

It was the summer of 1932. Lotti received a letter in the mail. Grandma asked Lotti to come for a visit during the summer. Lotti was very excited.

Lotti loved her Grandma, who lived in Miltenberg, Germany. Lotti, her parents and big sister, also lived in Germany. Germany is a country in Europe on the other side of the wide Atlantic Ocean. You can see a map at the end of this story.

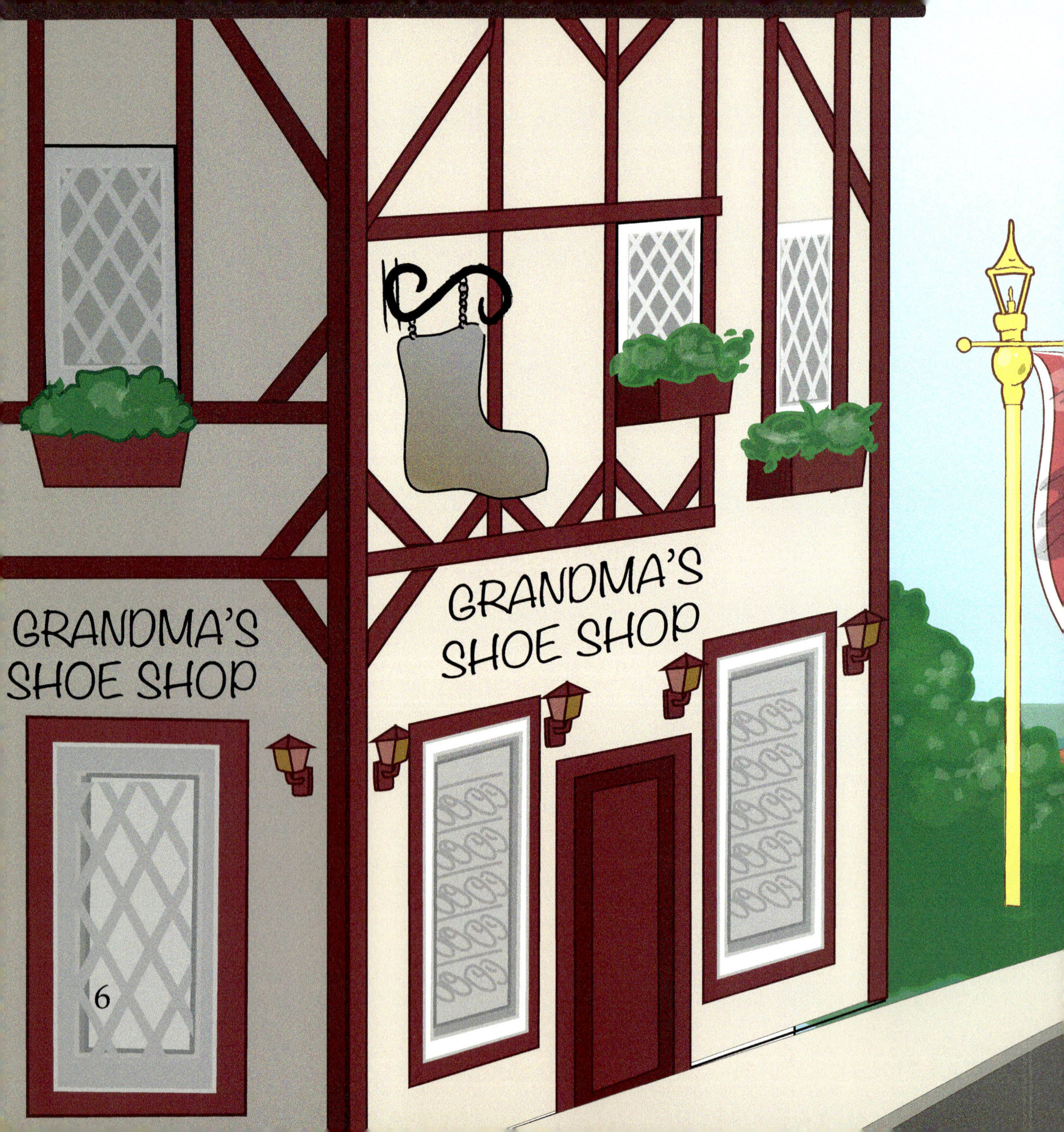
GRANDMA'S
SHOE SHOP
GRANDMA'S
SHOE SHOP

Lotti's Grandma ran a shoe store in Miltenberg. She was so busy that she had little time for anything but work. So Grandma let her grandchildren visit for a week, one at a time. During the day, the lucky grandchild could play without having to please the grownups.

Now it was Lotti's turn! She was happy to roam alone in the big forest at the edge of town, to go down to the Main River (sounds like "mine") to watch the tourist boats go by, and to swim in the river.

But even good swimmers, even grownups, had to be careful when they swam in the Main River. Parents in Miltenberg warned their children that the river was strong and fast. The powerful current could easily wash them away into the Rhine River and out to sea.

Lotti loved to swim. Her mother had taught her to be a very good swimmer. Lotti could do all kinds of strokes, and knew how to float gently on her back.

Elizabeth Lived in Miltenberg

Little Elizabeth lived with her family in Miltenberg, near Lotti's Grandma. She was smart and brave and thought she could go anywhere and do anything, even though she was only 5 years old.

Lotti and Elizabeth had never met. But they would meet soon . . . at the Main River.

Elizabeth Runs Out to Play

It was a lovely sunny day with a blue cloudless sky. The earth seemed warm and kind. It was just the sort of day when you want to walk or skip or cool off in the river.

"Elizabeth," said her mother, "don't go near the river. It's not safe. You're only 5 and you can't swim!"

"Don't worry, Mommy," said Elizabeth. "I'll be careful."

Elizabeth's big brother Eric decided to go swimming in the Main River. He told Elizabeth, "Stay at home with Mother. The river is too dangerous for little girls. I'll be back soon."

Poor Elizabeth! She felt hot and cross. Why must she stay home on such a hot day while her big brother Eric could cool off in the water? She decided to follow Eric quietly so he wouldn't see her. If he looked around, she would quickly hide.

While Eric walked to the river, Elizabeth skipped along at a safe distance behind him, watching her brother and hiding in the bushes so he wouldn't see her. It was exciting, like being a spy! Elizabeth felt the cool breeze from the river. She was smarter than her mother, smarter than her brother. They couldn't make her miss the fun!

Eric reached the Main River where there was a shallow area for children to play, and a deep place where big kids and grownups could swim. These areas were separated by ropes. There was a wooden walkway along the river to make it easy to go where it was safe to swim.

Eric climbed down the ladder into the cool water and started to swim. He didn't see Elizabeth, who was walking behind him, carrying a towel she had grabbed as she left home. It was a very pretty towel with reds and yellows and other bright colors.

Elizabeth remembered that Mommy told her to stay away from the river. But Mommy didn't say she could not jump and play on the wooden walkway at the edge of the river. Elizabeth would be careful not to fall in. She was a big brave girl! Why shouldn't she have some fun?

So Elizabeth jumped up and down and laughed while Eric swam farther and farther out.

Oh, no! Suddenly Elizabeth slipped on a wet wooden board. She fell into the river! Next thing she knew, the current had carried her into deep water.

Elizabeth tried to call for help. But the words would not come out! She didn't know how to swim and could not keep her head above the water. Water filled her nose and her mouth. She could not breathe or make a sound. Elizabeth was terrified!

She was being carried farther and farther from shore. None of the grownups had seen her. Eric didn't know she was there. Why hadn't she listened to Mommy?

Brave Lotti to the Rescue

Lotti was all by herself, playing near the Main River while Grandma was at work. Lotti could swim, but she was too smart and too grown up to play where it was slippery. Lotti made sure to stay safe.

Suddenly she saw a little girl struggling in the water holding a red and yellow towel. None of the grownups had seen the little girl. Lotti was afraid that if she looked away from the river to find a grownup to help, the little girl could go under the water and no one would be able to find her. Lotti knew it was up to her to help.

Lotti jumped into the river, clothes and all. She knew just what to do. Using all her strength, she swam to Elizabeth.

Lotti was smart. She did not get too close to Elizabeth, because Elizabeth might grab Lotti and both could drown. She told Elizabeth to hold tight to the towel and not let go. Lotti grabbed the towel and towed Elizabeth toward shore - to a ladder where they could climb out onto the boardwalk. But both girls were very tired.

Elizabeth could not climb the ladder by herself, and Lotti was too tired to help her.

A strong man saw Lotti rescue Elizabeth. He ran to the ladder and lifted Elizabeth up the steps. Lotti climbed up behind.

Both girls were safe!

Elizabeth survived that day thanks to Lotti. The girls now were friends.

And for a while they sent each other letters.

Lotti's Reward

The whole town of Miltenberg turned out to cheer Lotti. Newspapers reported the rescue of a 5-year old by a courageous 9-year old. People were happy for Elizabeth and proud of Lotti.

MILTENBERG Aug 05 1932

MAIN ECHO

Lotti Steinberger

A courageous 9-year old girl named Lotti was able to pull to shore, with the aid of a towel, a 5-year old girl named Elizabeth. It was a miracle for otherwise Elizabeth would have drowned in the swift current of the Main River.

Less than a year after the rescue, Adolf Hitler became the leader in Germany. He hated Jews for no reason, and he decided to hurt them. He said Jewish children could not go to German schools any more. But because someone in the government knew that Jewish Lotti had saved a Christian child, they let Lotti stay in her school with her old friends and teachers.

But soon Lotti's parents and their children left Germany to be safe from Hitler's hatred. They settled in Haifa, a city in what is now Israel. Lotti and Elizabeth lost touch.

A Happy Reunion

Many years later, after Lotti had died, her sister asked people in Miltenberg what had happened to Elizabeth. She was told that Elizabeth had married, had 5 children and 5 grandchildren, and lived in the German city of Munich.

One day, I went with Lotti's nephews and nieces to Munich. I had arranged to meet Elizabeth, now 85 years old. We had dinner together with one of her daughters, Henrike. And what do you think Elizabeth brought to the restaurant?

She brought the towel that Lotti used to save her. It looked like new, with bold, bright colors. Elizabeth and her family said they will never forget Lotti's courageous rescue.

Elizabeth leads a happy life, proud of her many children and grandchildren. None of them would have been born if Elizabeth had been swept out to sea. When Lotti saved Elizabeth, Lotti saved Elizabeth's whole family. That was a big, brave, important thing for a little girl to do.

The End.

NOW THAT YOU HAVE READ THIS STORY AND KNOW ALL ABOUT THE RESCUE, HERE ARE SOME ACTUAL PHOTOGRAPHS.

The beautiful town of Miltenberg where Grandma lived.

This is how Grandma's old shoe store looks today

The Main River in Germany looks calm here but it is dangerous for little girls

Young Elizabeth with her brother in the background

Lotti (left) and her older sister Judy before the rescue

Elizabeth, a few years after she was rescued

Lotti (left) and her older sister Judy, shortly after the rescue

Lotti age 12

Lotti as an adult

Elizabeth, now
a grandmother,
holding the towel
that saved her life

USA
Atlantic

GERMANY
EUROPE
Ocean